Poetry Lore

Kyle Lance Proudfoot

authorHOUSE®

AuthorHouse™
1663 Liberty Drive
Bloomington, IN 47403
www.authorhouse.com
Phone: 1-800-839-8640

Published by AuthorHouse   03/23/2012

ISBN: 978-1-4678-9607-8 (sc)
ISBN: 978-1-4678-9608-5 (e)

Poetry Lore

(Dedicated to my Mother, Greteke Lans,

who has always been there for me.)

Part 01

Mass Energy, The Death-Life Conspiracy

Kyle Lance Proudfoot ©

Do What You Want As Long As You Harm No One
Paganism: Celtic, Pagan, Wicca, Witchcraft

The Animal

I am the animal,

The Ground and the Sky

And the Waters and the Sun,

I am all.

I feel the earth beneath my bare paw,

Swimming the currents,

Flying the waves,

The vision of the Light I can hold,

I am the animal.

Mine is the current to make,

Eddy or whirlpool,

The matter is forged as I gesture

For all the energy is mine to wield.

I am all,

I am animal.

The Elements,

Our builders of substance,

Essences of form,

I am in touch with.

Like no other,

I am.

All that matter;

I,

King of this planet,

Ruler of all the matters,

Behold me!

I am Constructor

And Destroyer

With the might to determine it all.

Behold me!

I am the maker of my own fate:

I am Human . . .

Was This Life of Law And Good A Futile Effort?

Onslaughted and attacked the village did tremble,
Its innocence away, aswept in blood,
Evil Brigands throughout them had assembled,
The Cherland Town had been the fee that stood;

Of the evilest hearts, they were well known to be,
Of the women raped and the children killed,
Not a look of guilt did any one carry,
Of practice to Chaos, to the land they spilled.

Through the boiling blood of their victims, that did swell,
Of the pain they did thrive and shriek with joy,
Preaching to a foul Demon, from the depths of the Hells,
Corruption its tool, human man its toy.

But in the script of life, evil has no substance,
To be vanquished and destroyed, its lone fate,
Scattered to the wind, with a deathly dance,
Its power agone, then love to create.

So, is it mere coincidence suddenly Light was seen?
And that, oh noble a knight did ride?
Clad in full plate armor as though in a fantastic dream,
With scabbard and sword at bright shining side.

Was it just a fluke, that upon his nostrils a wind did pervade,
A wind that dost carry that deathly dance,
Beckoning the knight, blond flowing hair, in glorious serade,
Quelling his body beyond, to what lies thance.

And then upon the village, the truly man did come;
Silent vows of Vengeance, sacredly sworn,
As knight saw what a cruelty and pain, that had been done:
Remaining were only ashes forlorn.

'Who's to keep this rising evil suppressed, which so destroys?
How's peace to exist, so totally craved,
There but no remnant of good, must we remove these decoys?'
And as knight thought, he searched what could be saved . . .

But hope was to be lost until a small whimper was heard.
Upon that cherished sound the knight did speed,
To be revealed, surely a victim of evil cause
And knight presented hand with care fathered.

With poised stature and questioning voice, did ask the knight,
"Oh poor tattered man, what has occurethed?
What evil force wreaked such damage upon thy holmly site?
What creatures are so in evil bathed?"

To the word of the knight, the poor tattered man did respond,
"Why, oh noble, was a band of thieves.
The ones so renowned, you know, and oh what fortune that has dawned,
That I must no more under boards do grieve . . ."

The knight did then pause with etched and crafted splendor indeed,
Recall upon this group so known, he did.
To a Demon God they worshipped, off good they did feed.
Upon their sleeves a horned fly wear they did.

It was the cunning and mastery of wit, they loved
To trick a foe and then his fate to seal.
Many a band such as this had then donned a style of class
Where those arched brows increase their self-appeal.

Again, was it chance that did bring knight to glance upon sleeve?
With mind instinctively control taken.
Can there be much said of what the knight did likely perceive?
That a grinning fly did sit unmistaken.

"Poor tattered man, you hold the mark of that villainous group!"
Said the knight with excited inquisitiveness.
"Oh, why, yes I do, what a surprise," he said with a stoop,
"Thanks for pointing that out, you do impress."

As though from a crew of a stage conductor in total control
The silence that existed was broken.
From a tilt of a staff a chorus of a sound followed,
Action becomes the prime ruling token.

Erupting around the two came a score of tattered men.
With a voice caught in perfect glicendo
The poor-tattered man spoke again.
And his laughing made quite a crescendo!

"Why, my dear brothers . . . I do appear to have it don't I?"
He then beckoned with his hand to see what.
        "Do you agree my brothers, upon my sleeves, dost
              Appear to be a kind grinning fly!
                    Dost it not?"

With a laughter to douse even Chopin's soft, sweet tunes,
The motley crue did acquise to his words,
   "Why, righty right, you do!" One such one did say,
      "And by our own Mother's prune,
         We do too!"

With concealed fury, fist went white and breath did stagger.
The words that had spoken were words of true taunt,
Of great anger that welled from within, did cause to trigger
The flash of the furious to be sent.

Upon the gaunt throat of the sword the shining point did lie
And followed stinging words afilled with hate,
"Is thout who caused this anguish that spread heart with pain to cry,
Is this the torment that had been their fate?

Of the evil of Hell that was upon them besetted
Into thy soul shall that burdened be placed
And as thy tiny life crumbles you shall be the besetted,
Of your own tortures you will taste.

In his claws of black death thy stricken soul shall truly reach,
In the maw of the four clawed dragon ripped!
Thy soul shall be consumed by the very Demon you preach,
Utterly destroyed, life completely stripped."

"Now now, oh sacred knight of splendid words; they impress me so,
Who is to give this fate you proclaim?
If thout shalt look, may vision direct thee, your evil foe,
Awareness will then come true aim.

May I unto thy greatly stature pose a question one,
And through clear question may thick mist be cleared!
To allow light reach a hiding mind that does knowledge shun,
For the blocking gates that live to be seared.

Is it not true you hold a code of ethics, honor, and glory?
One that is held until death do you part,
You are not permitteth to harm the harmless art thee,
You may only claim the strong and stalwart.

Oh lordly honor bound soul, do we carry tools of death,
Do we have the weapons that you do bear?
Are we the scythe wielding ghouls whose fate lies on our breath,
Against thy raging mind how could one fair?"

On the knights true visage did color drain to ashen white
And once bold assured stance did fall asway
As knight hit upon realization of his stricken plight
Leaving a gaping hole of foul lies.

True to word and thought, impeccable honor did knight have,
Bound by unsurpassable rules of code,
Held in glory and proudness, the most revered, those most brave,
For a knight a true saintly life did bode.

It was though string was cut, faith was suddenly severed,
Resolute mind became a sudden field of insecurity and doubt,
'Was This Life Of Law And Good A Futile Effort?'
His thoughts rang the land throughout . . .

That day the blood of another honor bound knight sunk deep,
The core of the Earth shuddered and shrank away,
For a spreading rot was saturating a once divine keep,
Leaving few remnants of a good to stay.

That day the 'poor-tattered man' continued on with his men,
Of Evil slaughterings they did make rich.
On their doings of evil, they did thrive, wealth for all kin,
With joy and glee they made catch after catch.

But an incident to tell, he came on a group to quell
With Demon greed, his men out he did send,
But to unfortune an arrow to throat did blood swell
And his body corpse on the ground did end.

Yet, soul went on to the judgement plane and judgement was passed,
And open claws of black death did receive,
A soul evil pure, in glorious hell, reward to last,
To be Demon taken in an Asylum
Of no reprieve.

Time Energy

A Long Time Ago

I remember a time
When the wooden well bucket
Creaked.
It was winter,
Stormy, cold
Next to the sea . . .
I was lonely,
My Love had left me
The cold breeze,
It billowed, swept
Across our soaked landscape.
The soggy wooden barns
Lay along
Barren trails,
Lost without
Celtic Love,
In their stark
Naked parchedness.

Through Time

Time and Time lost,
Flow, Swirls,
Spirals.
Look through time.
Let your mind open,
Up to you.
Step Back.
Notice the Change.
Move forward into,
Vast regions of all time, spiral,
And places,
Where you can go
Never to be seen again
But by the Guardian of your soul,
Its keeper.
And all you know
Fade away,
And all you have seen
Vanishes,
Behind, before, away,
All gone,
And around you lies
The mysteries of all time
And you may witness them,
Now,
In the region of your mind
Where walks
No living soul
But your own . . .
And all else that lies
Where you have always been,
Where you shall always be,
But now,
Is always yours
Now, sees everything
Now, Is Here.
And you can see everything
Because you have stepped back
And allowed Your vision
To take it all in,
You have stopped straining;
Looking for something that is not yours,
Avoiding something that is,

Until you become cross-eyed.
Like the poor dog who has been hit,
Once too many times . . .
Let yourself go.
You won't fly away,
Or vanish,
Or lose or disintegrate.
There is such
A thing
As Gravity,
And Earth.

The Clock

Time only occurs in our minds.
The clock is the
      Measure of such subjectivity;
Time by itself does not exist.
       If you count 1, 2, 3, seconds four,
          That is what a clock is for:
              It gives us order,
              It gives us structure
              And restriction
              Time alone has no measure
              And that is it.

Spiral Energy

The Beginning of the Spiral.

And then the light is come.
There is a suddenness to this all,
A tempest, an unsurity, uncertainty,
An unequivocable feeling of
Out of control, no restraint,
Nothing barred, the road is
Free and I am on my way into the
Universe!

In to the Spiral

I want you.
Pulsate with evervescence,
Envelop me.
Take my nostrils,
Warm my face,
Echo over the layers of skin that
Bar me from your purity.
And protect me,
Oh protect me,
Pulsating white light
That fills my lungs with giving life,
Enter me and take me on
Your speedful voyage.
Your entity
Is the only
Power
That
Can
Hold me

Spiral Motion

Up and down we go, round and
About we fly, down to the ground,
Up to the sky, into the clouds
And out again!

Personal Spiral

Pain, Doubt,
How do I get in?
I want to
Have people admire me.
If people admire
Me me me me me . . .
I am not so decisive.
Me. I wish to move freely.
How to move freely?
I have tried inconspicuously,
But then no one noticed me
And I felt lonely.
I wish to have people notice me,
So I may ignore them.
And they think that is o.k.,
So I can be lofty
In their admiration.
And then I can swoop down
And take my pick
Of fresh carcass.
And eat it up,
Kiss it, lick it,
Clean it dry.
Fancy it with decoration,
And gain further admiration
For my artistic endeavour.
What was it that struck me
So powerfully?
By the maiden I saw today.
She was uncompromised.
She was wearing
An orange-pink dress!
In this day and age?

Body Spiral

On white plane of Black,
A black moon does shine,
This is the realm of
Opposite Polarity.

Envision not
The coiled dance of
Colored stream in
Time's endless voyage.

When is not an issue,
Agenda's do not exist,
Freedom is the answer
If you think you can persist.

Welcome to the Realm,
Of Opposite, and
Polarity, and of
Finitude and Infinitude.

Behold the plain
In tender grasp,
It is only
Yours for a short while.

Entropy, Energy
Are indestructible.
They will last forever,
Never touched by foolish hand.

On black plane of White,
A white moon does shine.
This is the realm of
Opposite Polarity,
It is all really the same.

Love Spiral

When I type, I try to reach GOD, when I write the words that flow out of me. It is a reason why my typing skills must, must improve . . .
What brings me here?
My quelling heart despair.

My everlasting internal fear and shadow.
From quoth to raven.
In the night air her voice howls out to me.
For naught the light.
My barren soul that doth twirl so.
For never more a poet's bore.
Oh, come dwelling night to my front door.
I let you in for ever more.
Nothing is a trifle to your.
Flaming face.
Feel not despair but triumph thy glowing heart.
The crescent wave that
Holds up time . . .
Oh, begone splitting gut.
You put my drenched.
Fall in a rut.

Now I call upon thee, the brave light of light.
Now you contest thy claim, one and all in the curdling vat.
I wish I could see you now, upon the floating heaven,
You demand such.
What is the bondage to be freed?
My cry is heard.
Answer! Oh, saintly bowels . . .
All I hear are growls,
Are they the warning of souls
That passed this way?
Answer!
Or be cursed to the toilet bowl!
I am at the brink of Despair, a heavy travelled place, I see . . .
Where everything is hopeless.
You are so hard to find in the mess . . .
Forget the Moriarte's, Or Socrates!
Give the everlasting word of Peace to this barren wasteland!
To the wandering souls . . .
That cry hunger in the night.

DO YOU GIVE US LOVE?

(Inspired by Edgar Allan Poe)

Female Spiral

Why must I make haste
            but tread slowly?
My progression has stopped me
            But
    Maybe, I won't have too ask for the answer
        I don't want to.
        I don't want to!
        I don't want to . . .
        Why?

        Why . . .
        Every night
            I am lost by what
        I know,
    I am slowed by the
            speed at which
                        I'm progressing.
        I live to die,
        I am purely impure
        And I am not I,
        I am frozen
        By these steps
        I make
        And
        I cannot
        Go
        Further
        Dying.

Male Spiral

I do not know what it is.
It looks like a gun,
It looks like insanity, an elaborate
Door knocker for the reclusive, something
To strangle your passions with, a
Demented persecution of our freedom,
Anguish, torment, foul corrosion,
A ronking form bagger: The trap
Of the typical betraying female . . .

Sex Spiral

I am so cool and she is so hot,
I wanna be a jock and stick it
Right up her.
Either way I am a Rock & Roll Star,
I will lean back as far as the
Down hill ski pole will go.
She will trot like a fox in flame,
We will shake our thing in rattle,
Hum, and rock and roll.
She will bounce her toosh and move her
Thing like a sweet kansas breeze,
We will pant in the sun's heat
While she spreads back for more air.
Like we are all Rock & Roll Star's.
It is a metaphor come true.

Mind Spiral

My mind, my oh my.
My oh my, I wonder why.
It is a wonder.
Maya everywhere.
Everyday, all the way.
It is with constitution.
No escape from form.
Its. It is. It is not.
Unapproachable.
Never the merciful.
Never free.
From Form.
My mind centered in.
Contradiction entered in.
Forever on and
On it.

Societal Spiral

. . . the dance of the dead, the dance of the dead: It is in my head, the frothing misery of the tortured mind in its withering gaze. No sign. No hope. This the tortured lot of all; it brings me down Insanity, in continual death, in continual death, in continual death. One thing after another, it never ends, it never ends: The dance of the dead, it never ends; It is in my head, I never thought it could get there but every day it comes, does not cease. I see the tortured lot of humanity and do not know whether to cry or shout. Is it partly my fault? I see it every day. I see it every day, I see it every day, the dance of the dead, the dance of the dead, the dance of the dead, the dance of the dead, how can they live like that?

Justice is lost, Justice is raped. Winning is all, find it so true, so grim, so unreal. This is my chance to get it out. This is my chance to speak, to speak, this is my chance to feel. Right. Right, left, this is my chance to scream out at the nonsense that is around me, this is my chance to scream! Do you see what I see? Do you feel what I feel? Do you see what I feel. Do you feel what I see? Don't get me wrong, it is that bad. Penetrate the smokescreen, I see through the selfish lie. A choice is made for you my friend. Or is it? "How did we get so far off track and why is it that I am on it more than others?" How can i be more on it than others? How is it that I hold a truth others do not and what are the ramifications of that? Why am I now more off it than others. I cannot see, I cannot hear, I cannot die, I cannot breathe, I cannot cry, I cannot breathe, I cannot die, I cannot believe this is happening to me if I knew what it was. How many people hold this vision and where are you . . . How many know what I know. What is it that is eluding from the truth. Am I progressing or decaying? Thank you for giving what I have, thank me, thank you, thank me, thank you, thank me, what am I struggling against? IF IT IS WITHIN ME WHAT IS IT? WHAT IS IT? WHAT IS WHAT IS IT? What is it?

The what is the agony that grabs at each of us after each word after the agony of Christ: Freshly killed. That is what every body feels after every statement. Just like dinner. Ready to pounce. Ready to kill upon the weak up'on the week upon the weak RAVISHED, TORTURED UPON THE RACKS OF HUMANITY, THE TORTURED VEIL OF SECRECY AND AGONY LOST IN YOUR MIND, YOUR LOSS BECOMES MY GAIN. ANGER, MISERY, YOU'LL SUFFER UNTO ME. Don't forget the pain, that anguish, in fact . . . relish in it, take it in and let it drive fear into your hearts, oh mortals! Let it drive the passion from your furrowed brow and the pride from your beating heart so all stop and you wrench in disgust away from this place of death. And do it quickly for there is not much time left . . .

Waves of fear they pull me under making my reality into there's. Everyone is after me, here them calling, hear them calling me . . . HAH HAH HAH, HAHrrrguh. Waves of Thunder, waves of thunder billow in my ears as I am dragged beneath into their warm embrace. Pull, Pull, pull, pull, pull AWAY! Don't get dragged in . . . Glug.

(Inspired by Dance Of The Dead and Mettalica and Alchoholics everywhere)

The End of the Spiral

And the light goes out, and
I am tired of the lights going out,
And the I will die of the anguish
Existing in the switch pulled down,
And I do not want the darkness
That then follows in the mystery
Of the night.
And the lights are pulled out, the
Life sweeped from me, the impenetrable
Folds that now vanquish in the
Oncoming, penetrable,
Piercing parrish of the night. Begone
Foul beasts, your time is yonder. In
Another dimension, not this one, not mine, not ever again.
Begone!
And do not step foot here again!!

Out of the Spiral

Keep on focusing, though your
Might may blur, leave the road
Behind, there is much to come,
Be clear, though I
Know you are confused now.

Love Energy

While You Breathe . . .

Keep the mind alive . . .
Strive for peaceful giving
And Love will be yours.

-maintain consciousness
-while you are in her ● get in touch with each other's energies ● a higher sensual
level of the body ●
-Love is sacrifice ● the giving of ones self ● it is only safe to do this with an
agreeable partner ● it creates a completed energy flow, a self-contained, high
intense energy flow, a closed circuit, if it is not closed, energy will be drained ●
after all this leads to the next point ● you intuitively desire self-sacrifice, for this is
a virtue taught, however it will cause ejaculation/orgasm ● the ultimate self-giving
will occur and this is one way to do it . . . ● better is to try to last as long as you can
practicing Taoism, it is not about the ejaculation but about the act of giving Love
itself . . .

Know not your suffers
As lack of happiness
But as forgiveness . . .

-bodily pains ● pains of the body
-forgiveness means before reward ● before you are given what you want ● energy
is moving, which is probably the definition of energy ● energy is motion ● if it is
blocked by tension, the anti-matter of motion, pain and tension will be felt ● during
sexual intercourse, there will be pain felt ● the usual idea is to endure ● relax, pain
will fade and you will be able to give and take what you want . . . ● rise to a higher
plane of energy with your partner

Embrace the power
Of energetic experience
And you have life . . .

-Life is something which can be held in ones hand, or actually had ● if you hold
onto it with your trembling hands and fingers you have power and energy, sort of ●
now embrace a powerful and energetic, completely bodily and mentally experience
● the tantric energy will rise ● you have life ● you are teaching each other to be ●
independent ● uncompromised ● to live is to love, to love is to live

Keep me alive with
Your lovely smile, don't fade now,
    We might go away . . .

-The perspective of a baby in his mother's arms

Romance Is A Dance

Romance is a dance
With the wild wolves when bitten
With mad utterance.

Flowing in the mind
Stream's eye, glowing for the love
Of one's devotion.

-In the particular sense, it is my eternal quest for greater experience, if such is not
clear, it is my continuing search to discover how I can more enjoy life ● the glowing
part is my belief it is working ● woh ● belief ● do not only believe ● see ● results, if
they are to be results, must be self-evident

Fleeing the need, of a
Feed that takes the soul to the
Place where we are freed.

-As we walk around, move around, from day to day, spot to spot, point to point, we
set up, or have already set up places where we can sustain our motion ● this is
called the feed ● it, unfortunately, is also a dependent, or becomes one ● it feeds
off of us in return ● all things react equally in return ● now here is sustenance
which will lead you to a better motion and the first step in discovering it, is to free
your feeding places

Take heed, yea who eats,
Feasts, on the animal's skin, kin,
Kind, for you will know
　　　his tortured butchered mind
　　　And agonize from your
Torture, captivity, and slaughterings
Of these millions of beasts . . .

Circle Energy

Smash The Father Raging Sky

(Death 01)

Cry!
Smash the Father raging sky.
Weep.
Die in Motherly anguish.

Faint the ever-oppression bestowed
Upon you,
Cling to the ever-barren rock of
Mortal despair . . .
Begone the vanquish of your
Earthly grave
And feel the hot sweat pouring down
Your veins . . .
Pulsating beneath the wet sky,
You cannot see,
Your clenching fists
Are clawing at my spine
And all its nerve endings,
Your mortal cry
Is resonating throughout the
Canyons
Of fathomless despair . . .

And you cannot do anything
But squeeze every ounce of pounding
Blood,
Which now holds you in its trembling
Heart,
Not the broken shards
Which once held together,
Now a shattered fate,
Life is hopeless and you had
Best not complain,
Speak not out,
Show not your
Pain . . .
Not to be released,
It is only yours,
Fool.

(Inspired by Charles Dickens and African Slaves)

This Is The Beginning

(Life 01)

This is the beginning . . .
In the birth from the womb,
In the conception from the tomb,
The dying grave is born new life
And time spins round
Like death to birth
To birth to death . . .
The light is on in your Mother's smile
And you fade away, drawn to her,
By him,
This is the end
And from all ends
Comes new beginning.

This Is The Way It's Done

(Death 02)

And no other way

Cause that is all, I have to say

And this is the way

It's done . . .

Now!

It's done!

And once again we

Try do to it some other way

But no other way

Can it be done

And this is the way it's done . . .

The Lesson Teaches Itself

(Life 02)

The Lesson teaches itself,
Such is the nature of life.
On and on, over and over,
So it will be learned . . .

The lesson teaches itself
And so it must be taught
As it contains its own answer,
So it should be learned . . .

The Lesson teaches itself
And the lesson is not learned . . .
The message is lost
And so the lesson is not learned.

The Lesson teaches itself
And all the teachers in the world
Cannot give the secrets of experience,
So it will be learned.

So, listen now . . .
It will be learned, the Lesson
Has just taught itself.

(Inspired by Pythagoras)

The Eternal Grapevine

(Death 03)

They,
Who are
Lost and gone,
Have no
Imagination,
But Frenchmen, who
With their
Awesomely
Inventiveness
Beneath
The Eternal Grapevine,
Swim in . . .
In willful abandon,
Recklessly,
While we never
Venture from the beaten path
And sink in the mud
Of a thousand million footsteps.

> The Frenchman is
> An individual,
> In the sea of faces
> Which swim before him
> (In the Ocean's of Time).
> He wants to drown
> His sorrows from seeing so many
> Lost in the second-handedness
> Of Collective Consciousness,
> He does not want to see it . . .
> So, he drowns his sorrows
> Beneath the Eternal Grapevine,
> His friend of Originality,
> His infinity,
> Forever on.

(Inspired by Frenchmen and Beer and Wine forever . . .)

There Is Anger In This Moment

(Life 03)

There is anger in this moment,
Tension to burn you alive,
Suspense overtaking your heart . . .
Anger in this moment,
Tension in here,
Alive,
Do not give in,
You just might
Regret what
You have done
To spur me . . .
You understand not
What is occuring,
Contemplate your fate,
I will mutilate
Everything you stand for,
Give in not and you will suffer
More for it . . .
This is better,
I can hardly
Contain myself!
This is the end.

Existential Glory

(Death 04)

This room is full of
Emptiness . . .
I can only see wild images
Of stark white bare
Angled sharpness
Against
The Crystal Sky . . .
The white, white
Barren sky,
The emptiness
Is overtaking me
In everything I face,
Emptiness . . .
Why, why,
Why can I not see wholeness?
Why can I not feel the wildness of my typing desk here?
My table sits in front of me
Like a rock.
I, now, already realize
When I search for Beauty
It but fades away
In the twinkle of a tear-stained
Sorrow filled Eye . . .
It is not hers which cries,
My dear one,
It is mine.
The bitterness of this world
Is too much, too bear,
So, I see not your
Beauty, my friend,
Only emptiness,
Only thee, my friend,
And I welcome thee,
Cold, bitter,
Resonant
Emptiness, my friend,
Now.

(Inspired by breaking up of relationships and hopelessness in so many)

The Storm Of Busses And Cars All Polluting

(Life 04)

Oh, I wonder
Why I cannot stand
The terrors which meet me each day,
First the alarm
Then the storm of
Busses and cars all polluting,
All commuting,
All keeping pace with
Something misunderstood, oh why?
My head hurts and
My back is aching,
I am in a knot and I ain't breaking,
Speeding faster
And faster in this
Crazy world where I somewhere have to go.
There is no time
To mope about
Or be comfortably numb.
I cannot stand the light of day
And the church bells are ringing.
But the burning in my heart
Keeps me awake . . .
I would really rather sleep
And ignore the pain
Of the suffering and shame,
Of my eyes which see it all,
To the shaking of my knees
And the teardrops falling to my feet.
I can only hold on to the dream
And hope it will not fade away
In the turning away
Along the way . . .
All I want is a place
To eat,
Where no one kills the children
Anymore . . .
Somewhere off in a field
The Gunner sleeps tonight,
Why?
And far from flying high
In the clear blue skies,

I am spiralling to the ground
Into the dark hole where I hide
Why?
There is a kid who had a big
Hallucination . . .
Making love to girls
In Magazines . . .
Can anyone love him?
Or, is it just a crazy dream?
I get off the bus
And feel pointless,
Vision blurred
With only stories to tell . . .
To sell, to hell
With time,
Magazines
And pornographic,
Slideshows . . .
I am a sad man
And I do not know where to go
In this lost misunderstood
World.
Why should I return those calls?
Why should I walk?
Why do I have to be late?
Why should I commute,
Debate, romance, talk?
Shock. Bingo! Bingo!
Make them laugh . . .
Make them cry . . .
Make the pay . . .
Make them feel o.k.,
Not now, John,
We have to get on with the film show . . .
Who cares
As long as the kids go?
Who cares
As long as the kids go?
Who cares?

(Inspired by Pink Floyd)

Oh, Beautiful Woman From The Sky

(Death 05)

I do not Strive
For fear of Challenge,
I do not strive
And I bow my head in shame
For all the faults I am to blame . . .
I do not object
For fear of being noticed,
For fear of being hated.
I feel frail
For all this waste I carry,
I dare not object
Thoughts of pushing weight,
Altering Fate,
The thought of Being Great.
For there are those
Who will despise
Though they hold no truth,
I will reap their hateful eyes
And cower in the glare
Of a thousand fires
Of no acceptance.
Beneath the collective will
I cannot be . . .
But I want to!
You see my fellow fool,
I am lost in misery
And this is why I cannot do
It.
This is why I starve my face and body
Because then is when I can die
And then is when they will not Challenge me.
And this is why, now I strive!
And bellow out my urgency
And break the rocks of bromide
'Til they are broken true.
No fiendish longing to . . .
No endearing doubt . . .
Hold fast to the sails mates,
There is going to be quite the storm,
And shatter the rocks of bromide
As we wash up on the shore . . .

Gleefully, I dance and play
In my summer's full time day,
Not a chance of misery,
Not a trace of docility . . .
Come now, all yee savage race,
Try to take my leveled brow!
Hah hah! Not a chance,
I have weathered your storm and dance
And stand tall and proud
Without acceptance
From your terrible dependance.
I am happy!
And free!
No more terrible dependancy.
So the sunshine shone and warmed me,
I lay there tranquil and okay,
Underneath a leafy tree,
Playing a soliloquy . . .
(What Fate had in store for me
I could hardly guess!)
"Oh, my Goddess, I know you do exist.
Would you venture to my place
And grant me romance?"
Then, I saw her dress.
My gosh, it was so finesse!
It curled and wisped around me
Entrancing me to accept . . .
I bid her a welcome,
Please come, please sit!
But she wisped and curled around me . . .
It was too late to know we kissed.
Oh, what did she say to me as I undid
Her flowing dress and kissed her lips
And neck until I reached her breasts?
She held to me and I to her
'Till time slipped fast away
And we did not rest nor pause
Until our final gasp.
I licked her lips and she bit mine
And we did not stop
Until we did it over and over again . . .
I loved her and she loved me,
We rose to the overhead stars
And fell back down again.
Until we could not go any further
We shared each other's caress . . .

It was in such a place,
Her soft warm skin and flowing hair
Above me, where I did fall asleep . . .
She left me in the morning.
What a waste! (I thought),
What a tortured cry . . .
Why did she leave me here?
I hear the raven's cry,
The anguished scavenger
Cries for any answer . . .
Why did she leave me?
Thunder, damn it! Tell me!
Shatter your roof asunder!
Leave my echoes of despair behind
So I may live longer
For I will surely die
If I know not her reason why,
(I thought despairingly),
I do not deserve this . . .
I do not deserve to cry . . .
I am as strong as any man . . .
This is not my cry, not my die
And please come back to me,
Oh, Beautiful Woman From The Sky.
I am empty, and the Sun, is too bright,
The night, is too long, and the song, is done.
I will never touch any woman again,
I will raise the stone and crush my brain,
Where did she go?!
She must have a lover somewhere!
Yes, such must be it . . .
She just wanted me for a fling.
Well, I do not deserve this,
Maybe, I am not worthy,
Maybe, it is anything,
Maybe, if I do not find out soon
I will bash my head and bust my skull right in,
Of course, then I could never see her again . . .
Oh, the turmoil, the agony . . .
I cannot go on like this, how can she?
She must not love me . . .
Yes. Such is it!
She just wanted me for a fling,
To clutch me and claw me,
So I will lose my face and cower in shame . . .
I guess, such must be it.

Yes! Such it is!
Well, I will show her,
The selfish Bitch!
I will get a double-barreled shotgun
And blow her brains away!
For daring to contrive such,
Daring to hurt me in such a sickly way,
I hate her! I am gonna kill her.
Give me a gun!
Then we will have some fun.
HAH HAH HAH!
Such must be it!
Such is what I will do
And over and over again . . .
Yes! Give me a gun!!
I will blow her damn . . .
She suddenly returns,
"Dear? What is it, what is wrong?
My sweet Love . . . I have
Brought some cherry wine for us, and
Why do you hold such a grimace, love,
With such an awful stick?
I have been gone all morning
In search of lovely drink,
Wine, my dear, lovely cherry wine,
Would you like . . ."
BLAM!!
I blew her up in one fell swoop,
She is dead, the cherry wine
Fallen over her, like Love, so sweetly red . . .
I did not like cherries anyway, (I thought),
And especially not on someone dead . . .
So, I took her bloody pulpy head
And thought
This will make a nice mantelpiece
Over the fireplace in my shed . . .
And the moral of this somewhat macabre story is:
So we continue to rape and plunder
And shake our silly heads
At the injustice of the World
When four women are killed everyday
By men and battered every 18 seconds
In the U.S.A alone . . .
We are all guilty of crimes beyond belief
But it is this Misogyny
(The Typical Male Thinks With His Dick)

Which is encroaching to engulf all Love, Beauty
And Sexual Pleasure.
So, if you laughed or got a hard on
When he blew up her pretty head,
Remember, you are a Typical Male Primate
And got a hell of a lot to set straight . . .
Work for your independence
And integrity,
Power from your Spirit and Soul . . .
When you hold a Fairy Queen
In your tender grasp
And she leaves you afterwards,
Remember, nothing always lasts . . .
Neither do you.
Do not destroy yourself or relish in the past,
It is part of life's mysteries,
Something you cannot grasp.
Or, it is as simple as Love,
Cherry wine, which you may have,
To know you drank
From her over-flowing stream,
Taking some, giving some,
A lovely dream . . .
You can know you will have Freedom,
If you bravely go on,
Such is True Love,
And someday, you will meet again . . .
If not in this one
Then in the next one . . .

(Inspired by Consolidated)

I Saw A Merry Fisherman

(Life 05)

Oh, I saw a merry fisherman
Who waltzed one day!
Oh, I saw a . . .
Round little tidbit of a
Circular solid jam,
I squeened in adolescence
And left it at the seem
And now I am here.
Hee Hee Hee . . .
Arrrggh matey, I am here
And as happy as can be . . .
I am a storyteller,
A Botty Geller,
An unsulurpuprous
Noobie Creamer . . .
Blllurp!
I stick my tongue at you
And what are you gonna do?
With those incy icky tiddy widdy
Wonderful droplets of goo . . .
Oh, I saw a merry fisherman
And what arrre ya gonna do?
HAH HAH!

Foolish Mortal Of The Transient Flesh!

(Death 06)

How Dare You Foolish Mortal
Of The Transient Flesh!
Come To Me!
Evade Not My Consciousness
Mortal One
Who's Days Are Numbered
And Who Cannot Bear
The Stone Of His Own Making . . .
Yes! It Is Me Who
Perches So On Your Life's Work,
Who Now Demands Your Retribution
For Your Self-Righteousness
Which Has So Overwhelmed You
And Given You The Audacity
To Create This Foul Thing
Which Has Destroyed So Many
Creatures!
Yes, Creatures My Fiend.
All Those Lying Now
Bloodied And Dead Under Your Barren
Life!
Yes, Life My Fiend.
You Had Dare Taken It
To Uplift Your Own In Wanton Glory.
Now Pay
Foolish Mortal
Who Clings So Desperately
Now To His Creation . . .
Who Has A Rock Of Sorciphol
For A Gut.
It Is Pay Back Time
Brother . . .
And I Am Here
To Peck Your Eyeballs Out
Brother . . .
You Cannot Hide.
And To The Planes Of Hell
I Will Send You,
Never Meet You There . . .

A Dark Enshrouded Temple Parlor

(Life 06)

Dark enshrouded Temple parlor,
Despair in troughs of faded color,
Sin to follow, blinding grasp,
Reckless abandon, tangled past,
These are the stories which men call their lives
But little do they know it . . .

Do You Have The Key To Your Own Happiness?

(Death 07)

Dreadful,
Painful,
Sorrow full . . .
Empty,
Questioning,
I don't get it . . .
Why?
What is wrong with you?
Do you care?
Do you know?
Do you even want to?
Or would you rather just
Sit in your own
Tiny space
And fornicate
In the sheer delight
Of all of it,
Of the spite and Strife,
Hate and anger,
And the fight,
Then you regret . . .
A time of mourning
And you stretch
And struggle
To break free.
To break free
Of your *own* bonds,
Bonds of your *own* making.
Do You Have The Key
To Your Own Happiness?

The Vines In A Past Dream

(Life 07)

Puzzlement,
Decay,
Continual,
Circular motion,
Jagged motion,
Punch, turn,
Punch, collapse,
Collapse.
Collapse,
Decay,
Blindness, decay,
Groping in the twilight
Of the shadow
Of a forgotten day,
Gaping maw
Of hope lost
Beneath the tidal wave
Of eager insurgence,
Entrapped
Within
The tidal pool
Of overwhelming
Undercurrents
Which are your life,
Which bring you down
And if you would
Just stop kicking for once
And release your tension,
You might not be so heavy
And be victim to
The unconscious
Flailings of your feet.

So I Sit In This Dungeon Room

(Death 08)

So now, since I sit in this dungeon room
I can resume . . .
What is it about people
Which puts them into
States
Of inescapable fear?
And with it despair
And the humanity
And then with this excuse
Pretend not to know,
Until eventually
They do not know
And continue in careless abandon . . .
What makes them
So determined
To destroy themselves
And the world?
What makes us
Addicted to death?
What is stifling
Our every breath?
What are we to do
About our shrouded faces . . .
What causes it?
What brings us
To certain collapse?
Is it just nature,
Can so many people
Choose death?
At 300 per hour . . .
Or, is it just what they do not know
And have seen nothing else . . .
Or, is it the nature of the body
To desire death . . .
Is it the way we stand,
Slouched over and down . . .
Or is it our negative mentalities
Each and every day
Watching such atrocities?

Live Of Life Not Death

(Life 08)

Jesus Christ?
Live of Life not Death.
Take Your Sustenance
Alive, not decaying.
The seed holds the life:
It grows into the tree.
Do not eat the Human flesh,
It is of the cannibal.
Do not take your Sustenance
From Human flesh,
It is from the cannibal.
Would you eat something
Which is in poison and decay?
Would you eat something
Which is rotting?
The Flesh of the Human,
It is of the cannibal.
If there is no life
To feed it, it is degenerating.
Eat not the flesh of Human,
It is from the cannibal,
It is decaying.
Even if you are hungry or starving
Do not eat the flesh of Human,
It is of the cannibal,
It is rotting and decaying.
All must fade away . . .
All must return . . .
So Life would have it.
So Nature will do it;
As you eat the decaying
Piece of Human flesh
You are eating
Each and Every
Bacteria
And Virus
Which is
Feeding
Off of its remains . . .
Just like you are.
Do not ingest Death,
For you will surely die,
A most horrible and tortured demise.

Ride The Wave Of Your Own Momentum

(Death 09)

Competence
And all which succeeds
At creation . . .
Thought, Concept
Design, Formulation,
Completed Enjoyment.
Ride the wave
Of your own momentum . . .
(You will stir the hearts of others)
Fly by the speed of your thoughts,
Move by recurring surges
Each creating and supporting the next ones.
Break new ground,
Reach dizzying heights,
Powerful
Energy Release,
Creation!
Convince, Impel,
Inspire, Fly!
Enjoy!
Never tire
For you are always setting new ground
To work on,
New planes of existence
All supported by the previous ones,
In successive growth,
Never to fall
Or fail.
It is impossible!
You are assured,
By one step at a time,
One beat after another,
You will live
Even beyond this one . . .

This World Has No Hope

(Life 09)

This world has no hope,
It is a blackened hole
Of hardened feces,
And fossil fuel madness,
It is a black wallowing
Of doubt, frustration, and torment.
It is a deepening pit
Of cruelty, torture, and death.
It is lacking in life and beauty
And enough hope,
It is run by totalitarian
Headmasters and thanes
Who whip on their minions
Without respite,
With evil intent,
With selfish greed.
They curse the masses
To eternal enslavement.
You can do what you want but,
But not really,
You can smile and appreciate values
But do nothing about them.
Peace and happiness
Does not exist here,
Of Body and Mind,
All facets are dimmed,
All freedoms do not exist,
Obey the law and survive,
Protest and die.
My friend, do as we tell you . . .
And then someone tells me
This is the way it was meant to be
And do not worry
Be happy . . .
So, I kill him.
And then they whisper to me
This is the way it was meant to be
And they want me to pray . . .
So, I kill them.
I am a loner,
I am a rebel,
I am an outlaw,

I am now just a Jailbird
Who wants to be set free . . .
This is the way it was meant to be
And I can do nothing about
Society and its pains,
The masses and the peoples,
All of them billowing about me,
The riders in the storm . . .
I stand, the eye of the hurricane
And see it all . . .
Is it a teardrop which has
Fallen from my cheek,
Or, is it the rain
Of bitter sorrow . . .
I ask no one
And then someone tells me
This is the way it was meant to be . . .
I look at him
And he says,
"You cannot look anywhere but your own soul
And all else is darkness,
And all else is death,
And all else is random,
And it is your Self
Who is the maker of your Fate.
And it is only you
Who can set yourself free . . .
Be it from this Hell or another
It is only you
Who can set yourself free . . .
And this is the way it was meant to be . . ."
I look at him, once again,
And say, "Thanks,
I think I will be
On my way . . .
It was nice talking to you,
I hope things are O.K.,
I think I will leave
This birthplace, my birth Planet,
Which now seems so alien.
I hope you do fine.
Me, I will now
Do my best
To be
Now Here.

(Inspired by Neil Young and Jim Morrison)

Life Is Enjoyment

(Death 10)

And I live and die
To be happy, to succeed,
To prosper, to enjoy
All the richness,
And liberosities,
Which life and death can give,
To be free and in peace,
If life is taken and death stolen,
If the effort is made to do
What one has been aching to do,
If the effort is made to be
What one has been aching to be.
Warmth, wholeness,
Flow in solidity
To a graspable existence,
The only one I can live and die for.
Life is my own to live and die,
To live in my own Body, and enjoy it.
To live in my own Mind, and enjoy it.
To live in my own Spirit, and enjoy it.
To live in my own Soul, and enjoy it.
Life is enjoyment,
Life is satisfaction,
I take life and I live it.
And fight and battle to the very last death.
Breath of using action
Which leaves wisps of passing currents
In my wake
Of upward stance,
Releasing the undesired
And I grow lighter
With each exhalance
Pushing me farther . . .
My only fuel now Light
In the After Life
Freed from the material bondage,
Pushing me into eternal motion . . .
Into genuine Immortality.

(Inspired by The Beatles and Theosophy)

All The Things I Like

(Life 10)

Terrific hot sun shining warmly down upon me.
Drinking cold thirst-quenching slushes.
The cooling drops of a sprinkling shower on a humid day.
The happy purr of a cat lying quietly in my soft warm lap.
Wonderful attractive gardens displaying small colorful flowers.
Squirrels scurrying about, gathering nuts for winter supplies.
Having a birthday with lots of money and many good friends.
Playing soccer when your goaly saves every goal.
Listening to great music at loud volumes.
Winning, winning and winning again.
A great challenge which I succeed at.
Getting drunk and making a lot of rude jokes.
Loving her in the heat and the sweat of the night.
Remembering all the great times we had.
Living in the glory of my victories.
Walking through a plane of white and blue icy coldness.
A really hot bath or spa . . .
It is not if, when or where you die, it is not how you die,
It is how you lived your Life.

Part 02

The Power Of Release

Thank You Mom

This is a poem to you,
You who
Touches my sparking heart
And holds me in a bow.
With flowing embrace
The night flows
As the Light through a streaming window.
Where is fright?
You of amber gold and blackened bright?
Your sight is on me.
And it is nowhere.
Nearby, you will bring me to a park,
Your charm of eternal grace
Keeping me near.
This is you,
You who
I am writing this poem to.

In Return . . .

Something nice . . .
Something impossible.
Maybe a Romance.
Ballad, not a tragedy;
In constant stanza,
Form, and easy?
I do not know . . .
It seems gross.
Something pleasant
To help you relax.
No mental penetration,
No revealing of facts:
This has been done,
Now, to its best.
I will start.

Whistle, whisper through the land . . .
Wide, open, open and wide,
Gray rocks as far as to see.
The wind sweeps, billows, roars, flies,
Soars, whips through you and around,
Through you and around, crisp,
Strong in your face and body.
Sky all around, far as to see.
All the clouds, far out to sea,
Rolling, rolling and rolling.
Wide open, you can see the
Rocks stop at the beach. You are
On the shore of sandy beach,
Still the sky and windy air,
Now sand through your feet, around,
To the left and right, you see,
Water in front entirely.
Frothing waves rising, falling,
Crashing at your feet you twirl,
Rising and falling with wings.
Through the sky, up and down, to the earth,
The sea grows and grows, the beach,
The land, grows, rocks get larger,
Faster, faster, and you Crash,
Explode through the water. Waves
Return to motion as you
Dive into the depths of the

Ocean, deep into the depths
Of the water, to the bottom,
Where pearls grow silently.
Nothing can be seen here for
Your eyes, only presence deep.
And you stop, stop and feel it.
Probing deeper, and deeper,
Floating, you feel it go on.
You cannot pinpoint any.
Nothing blocks the way here
Except occasional caves.
All around, wide open, now
Surrounding your being, how
Supporting, raising aloft
On the dense, slow moving waves
Beneath your feet, your back, then
Lifting, and slowly you flow,
Going deeper and deeper
To the beginning of this
Waves cycle . . .
Now the whole sea.
Moving with its momentum,
Faster and faster we go,
Repeating, ungraspable,
Determined, directional,
Feeling the pressure softly,
Gaining greater strength, with all,
Embracing, approaching it,
Continuously, forward,
On and on, always through,
With ease of motion, held by,
The unbreakable pressure.
Pending realease of this, with
All the others now nearby,
We fly faster than we have
Ever, fathomed to the deep
To get her, to get her, down
We go, we go. Here we go
To the ocean floor, where no
One has ever been before,
To see the Queen if she is in . . .
With a ripping roar we reach
The threshold of the deep, deep,
Deep, everlasting deep, where we
Can eat, maybe sleep and pause,
Forever, in her embrace.

Here we are, we have escaped,
We have returned, to find her
Sequinely upon the sand,
As we fly with the wave and
Roaring wind of deep gained
Desire, impounded in one
Quest for Equal Return.

And on we go, happily,
The sky again, open and
Wide, all around, landing on
The Earth and sand, warm in hand,
We kiss and lie down again,
To make further creations.

(Inspired by Atlantis and the Sea Queen)

Your Life Fire

Fight for life.
Fight for breath.
Fight for the
Upper region
In you chest.

Fight for air.
Fight for flight.
Fight for life
And all which is light,
Yet intense.

Fight for high.
Fight for sky.
Fight for the
Fire of Freedom
All the time.

Don't you rest.
Don't you rest
Until you sleep
And you have fought
And got the best.

Which you can.

(Inspired by Chronic Bronchitis and Asthma patients like my Father and myself)

POWER TRIP

I trust my flow:
Take me where I have to go.
Purgatory period is over . . .
All is burnt;
The fire is over,
The candle has been lit,
Now we can sing,
Next to the milestone
Of ancient heredity.
Not it is time
For Power,
Over all
Which is yours.
And will be
For those who have endured,
Have not walked over others.
Release for the good
And death and agony for the evil.
Justice served.
That is just how it will have to be:
No other way.
This is the time period
Where such will occur.
We will now regain
The land which is rightfully ours,
By not even taking it;
It lands,
Right back in our hands,
Once again free,
We can do what we want.

(Inspired by Native Indians and other enslaved Civilization's in History Of Humanity)

All Things

All Things,
To Balance : Stability,
Work in Circular Motion,
Balance Points are Centre of Spheres,
Are in Continual Motion,
Forces Enacting upon them are a result of Own Interaction,
Are Based on Interaction of Two or More Spheres,
Are Physical.

There are No Abstracts,
Just Inconceivables and Unnoticeables,
Which Can be Conceived of And eventually Noticed.
All Laws are Obviously Demonstrating Themselves,
In the World Around us,
Within us and Between us.

This is a Continuum of Flowing Energy,
Manifested in Different Forms,
Based on the Work Towards Balance,
Cause and Effect, Repulsion and Attraction.

We Are Capable of Comprehending All,
Of the Universe, Everything,
And Relating It to other People.

On The Same Street

Isolated systems,
Separate trajectories,
Never merging,
Crossing,
Affecting each other.

Isolated systems,
On the very same street,
Parallel momentum,
Bound to never meet.

Flying through time,
In the same direction,
Different beginnings,
Different destinies,
Temporarily abreast,
Then passing by.

Only Vision,
Recognition,
No binding forces,
Upon your thing,
Called life.

So, it is possible
To be happy,
While others starve,
On the very same street,
Cause I did not
Cause it.

And I never will,
I am not involved,
Only Mass destruction . . .
But such will not occur
While there are still
Good people afoot.

Making things for each other,
Lending a hand,
Giving a smile,
Making love,
Working for the promised land.

So now it is
Only up to me,
To decide
What I want
To do.

If everybody does
What they want,
We will have everything.
Free Enterprize rules!

It is all separate,
Believe it or not,
On the very same street.
This is why cars do not hit . . .
And you get
Where you want to go . . .
Safely.

Progression Over Planes

Spiralling is the Energy Flow of the Progression Over Planes.
Each Plane is a Complete Circuit, a Circle.
To Connect to the next Plane, you draw a line from each Circle to the next.
Thereby, you achieve an overall motion of the Spiral.
The way to go through the Connection Point is the Point where Beginning meets End,
Where they are the same,
Where Breath meets Breath,
Where the Circle Repeats,
From one Cycle to the next,
Through the Cycle of the Universe,
The Traversing of each Plane,
From Beginning to End and Around Again,
Forever on the way,
To Travel the Universe,
The Way to see all Time and Space,
Circle,
By Remaining Intact.
Circular,
Conscious of Each Cycle,
Each Plane.

Travelling Song

Dream a Dream,
A thousand Dreams.
Leave the face
Of outer realms.
Dwell
In caves,
Of revealing tales,
Of ancient past
And secret ties . . .
Release those chains,
Covalent bonds.
Enter the vast darkness
Of eternal embrace,
And dream the dream
Of a thousand dreams.
Face the night,
The sustaining deep.
Fear not death,
It is only terror.
What are you afraid of?
Are you guilty?
Then face the reality.
Let your body flow,
You are all body,
Go with it . . .

(Inspired by Out-Of-Body Travel and Lucid Dreams)

MY DREAM

I stomp through the bitterly cold morning dew . . .
It flies from my steel boots, miles away,
Chillingly cold bitter wicked morning,
Steel Boots!
What a stupid invention,
I venture to my horse, sword drawn,
Dew flying,
Something comes this way,
Bitter stone cropped wet cloud covered morning,
Onto my horse and off, we fly away!
This is my dream,
Do not venture or get lost in it,
It is dangerous . . .

(Inspired by Roleplaying Adventure 3D Games)

Lost In A Lonely Romance Wilderness Of Pain

The unconscious flowers lie,
Floating in the stream,
Twisted stems stunt their glory,
Down the sightless dream.

They do not know the currents,
Do not know the waves,
Blind to the passing events,
They go down in days.

Cluttered in dumps by the shore,
Cut off of the Earth,
Not one has known a Mother,
Weakened fragile birth.

The unconscious flowers rot,
And wonder in pain,
Everyone is a despot,
Each one is alone.

Some make it up to the banks,
Then dry in the sun.
Each lost one finally sinks,
No Evolution.

Death frees them from the River
Of Unconscious Flow,
The Universal Matter,
Back to roots they go.

Oh why, must there be
This tangled horrible task
Of treachorous pathway
And unseemingly ending mask . . .

Why can't we just know all of it?
Why can't we just do all of it?
Why do some lie in bitter distress,
And others enjoy Romance?

If we all come from
Tiny amoeba,
To cat, to ape, to human,
Why do some kill, murder and rape?

Is it just evolution,

Then what is the difference?
If it's just ignorance,
Then we will all reach bliss.

What is this whole mess?
Why can't I do anything?
If it's just been ignorance,
What's the purpose?

It is stupid.
There is no point to any of this.
Just completely random direction,
Which we call decision, but really it is chance.

It's not fair, I have happiness
And the potential to progress,
When my neighbour is stopped and hampered,
Just because of instinct?

It does not make sense.
What's the Purpose?
There is no nothing
And yet, there should be.

This is not just each person.
This is the entire Universe.
There is apparent progression:
We learn.

There is no significance
Until we gain Consciousness,
Then the Desires give.
But what are those?

The unconscious flowers flow,
As everything follows its design,
And pattern, in warm embrace,
In the waters of Time.

Do we reach for Eternal Salvation
Or physical relevance?
It is one and the same
For Paradisical Deliverance.

But if such is the point:
Why would we not have it already?
There is no judgement
In infinite Space and Time.

Why would there be laws?
Which entrap us?
Made to be broken?
Once learnt?

Break on through to the other side,
No one here gets out alive.
There is nothing nice about death.
And there is no point to life.

So, let's be in existential
Twisted agony.
And do whatever we please,
And do whoever we please.

And rape, and murder, and pillage,
Anything we desire,
Cause life has never treated us nice,
And all we've wanted are answers.

And the bitch who says 'No',
Just because of some excuse,
Fuck her over
And get what you want.

Cause if you don't get what you want
You'll never be happy.
Well, if you ask me,
Such is worse than death.

You got to do what you want
As long as you harm no other.
You are only responsible
For what you cause.

You will not be blocked
If you do not block another,
Another is anything besides yourself.
Yah, it's fucked up, but this is how it works:

I'm not worried at reaching happiness
Anymore; I know what I cause.
And, I know what I please,
And, I'm gonna get it, in the end, completely even . . .

(Inspired by The Doors and C.G. Jung)

"Collide-A-Scope Worlds"

Come on down man
To the resting place . . .
Somewhere where you
Can regain your face.

Money's good, money's right,
Money's gonna buy your food tonight,
Money's a product of your energy,
How much do you have?

Would you like to live in fantasy only,
Live on its shore,
Wanna know I'm alright . . .

Next to the shore in solitude,
But not alone, with you,
Watching the planets whirl by
In their kaleidoscope vision.

It is so easy to make a mess,
So hard to clean it up:
So easy to destroy,
So hard to create,
Must be a law of gravity;

Everyone is in some agony,
Mostly over their own fate:
Pessimistic visions and observations
Really suck.

You have to fight.
The difference in direction
Between good and evil
Is with the good the fighting gets easier
And with evil, it just gets harder and harder . . .

Worshipping on all levels
Is gradually fading,
From an Immortal, to a Priest, to a Politician,
To a Rock Star, to a Writer,
To a desktop fool, to yourself:
Finally freedom.

It's fun to say anything
And damn the consequences,

This is easy in a position
Where you know you will not hurt anyone
Or even mislead them.
The trick is to be clear,
Eloquence is Poetry
In a measure of such clarity.

It is fun to say what you want
When it is not directed at anybody.
You can.
What's the matter with rambling
Consequences?
Knowing somebody will read this:
Tempted to give it to someone;
It is so easy to destroy,
It is so hard to create.

When things break down,
It is so much fun to watch.
But it is so hard to rebuild,
Consequences of random thought.
So, some don't even get involved,
Decided it is not worthwhile.
It is only worthwhile for those
Who desire it:
Then it is quite the trip.

With good intent much damage is spared:
Picture 12-year old without Father,
Passing comment, torn and marred,
Now, forever scarred . . .
Don't get it?
Boy takes pride in achievement accomplished,
Passing friend crudely remarks,
Never tries again . . .

There is no such thing called Death.
Death is not release,
Death is transition,
Death is spiritual,
Death is reincarnation:
A gift from the Universe,
The gift of new life
Stamina, Beauty,
Oppurtunity:
A new body with a new face.
It is the Universe's way
Of saying it likes you . . .

After all, you have aged,
Birth brings refreshment.
But don't take it lightly
Cause an Effect remains.
It is a remarkable gift.
Personally, I hope not to age,
To remember all those things
I have done. Maintain my Youth
Forever and live happily ever after
Into true Immortality . . .

(Inspired by Time, Near-Infinity, Infinity and Immortality)

Your Land

You got to *except* who you are.
You got to *except* who you are and your position.
You got to accept who you are and all which is true and good:
You got to go up from here.

It's lower down than you think.
It's lower down than you think but it's where you start.
It's lower down than you think, you fall if you do not build.
Just let yourself sink down.

Are you going to drown?
Are you going to drown your abilities?
Are you going to drown and lose it all forever:
You know there is land.

Come to reality.
Come to reality even if you die.
Come to reality even if unhappy:
Let Gravity.

Let Gravity.
Let Gravity take control of you.
Let Gravity bring you to the Earth:
Earth to you.

Hit the land.
Hit the land hard with your feet.
Hit the land 'till you know its beat:
Your land.

Step on.
Step on the wide open *plane*.
Step on the impenetrable ground:
Down.
Down.
Down to the Earth you have gone.
Down to your worst you have fallen.
On.

Now. Now you can climb,
Only now sustainable . . .
Now climb, climb
And never fall
On blocks of solid reason,
To the ethereal tower in the everlasting sky.

Knight In Shining Armor

The Knight Cries
In Wet Shining Armor.
Whether from Blood or Tears,
It does not matter.
They are one and the same
To his Pale Blue Beating Heart
Which has gone through
The Ravages of Time
And Suffering.
Can he one day
Shed his Armored Chest,
His Covered Head?
And Fly with the
Winged Champions
Of Avalon.

Pearl World

And if you don't
Take a chance
On this pearl world,
You'll lose this
Diamond
Forever
Girl.
With our feet upon the floor,
Stomping the good old beat,
With my feet upon the floor,
I don't have to eat.
With my head up to the sky
I can breathe.
With my hands in the waters
I can create
My body to fly on the wind.
So, let's touch the skies,
And feel the earth,
And dance in the circling stars.
Spiralling eyes,
I think I see you . . .
You don't physically die,
You need your body.

(Inspired by homeless people of all kinds)

All I Wanted

All I wanted
Is a farm born girl,
Is a farm with her,
Not one with animals
For food.
A farm with her,
Lots of flowers.
A farm born girl,
In the field,
On the ground,
Not muddy.
A farm with her,
Green and yellow.
A brook to
Love her in.
Love her in,
Love her in,
Love her into your life.
To your life,
To your life you want to go.
You want to go
To her life,
On the beach,
In the woods,
Within reach.

All I wanted
Was a farm born girl,
Was to live in harmony,
With Nature,
On the farm with her,
With self-sustaining
Unending sustenance.
Why can't we have it?
Why can't we have it?
Why can't we have it?
Why don't I?

(Inspired by Vegetarians)

I Think I Need Love

All my life
I have believed in myth,
Medieval romance,
Destined.
Is the world
Black and White
Without?
I have been told
To find a bride . . .
I yearn to
Touch *my* bride,
I ache for you . . .
Lost without romance
In my stark naked parchedness.
I have been told
Light is the result
Of gentle kiss,
The caring hand
Lent,
A Touch,
Such loveliness,
In your smile,
It is for *me*?
I fall back
And sleep.
Am I to find you
To find myself?
Is it true,
Care given,
Is care returned,
Received,
And all is well
And alive . . .

Until we meet again
I will believe
There is such a thing
As Fantasy come true . . .

(Inspired by so many fantasy notions about Romance and Love)

You Will

The life you have lived
Has passed long,
You have fought the Good
Fight for your song,
You had faith in Truth
And all which is Good,
Whatever such might be
You have stood your ground,
You took the blows
To bloodied face,
And bruised your hands,
They froze and burned,
The tears tore down,
Your breath went shallow,
You heaved your blood
And still stood your ground.
You believe in Good.
Your intent is Good.
You fight for Good . . .
And live to tell.
What makes you different
From the others?
I Love you my love
And forever too.
If you ever doubt
The path of Truth,
Just take a look . . .
At the rewards.

(Inspired by Truth in opposition to the prevailing Lies Of Satan everywhere)

Coming To . . .

Beautiful,
Supine,
Divine,
Serendipitous,
You sit
So eloquently,
With grace . . .
Finely
Chiseled,
Perfect mold
Tight woven,
Pattern
Never diverging,
Your skin shines bright.
Your bones reflect
Strength, instilled
Balance, gained
Equinimity,
Flexibility . . .
You could not be better,
Unless you were Light.
But thank Fate
I may hold you
In this form
Of pure sensuality
Where our beings meld
And all our driven matters
Dissipate
In the fusion
And heat
Of our combined
Beings . . .
Goodnight . . .

(Inspired by the correct Eastern Taoistic Tantric Sex which the West is mostly
oblivious to)

You and I

"This fuckin' society
is destroying all which is good and true."
And so I am
By saying it does not exist
In this society.

I saw
A Maiden
Just now.
She was walkin' her small little dog
On St. Clair in Toronto
And she looked
Into my eyes
Like she knew the
Trouble I was going through.
I looked into hers
But the glare was too much,
Too bare.
She is
So beautiful,
Fresh and clean,
Like a once new summer's breeze,
Can you imagine us
Going to green flowered field,
Where there are trees,
And flowers and birds,
And no dirt,
No bugs.
And we would,
Have a blue sky,
With white clouds,
And a blue ocean.
And we would look into each other's eyes,
Without hesitation,
Fear, Evasion,
Doubt, Pain,
Illusion,
Right into each other's eyes.
No masquerade,
Just you and I.

(Inspired by dreams of the ideal relationship)

Gates Of Dawn

Here we go,
You and I.
We is going to the mountaintop
And beyond,
I like this flow, you make me
Feel all right.
I've never felt this way before . . .
Same to with you?
All right! All right, man!
We're going, going, going,
Coming, coming, coming,
Back and forth,
Like in time, in time, in time,
We are exploring the Universe
In time, in time, in Time,
We are exploring the Multiverse
In time, in time, in Time.
And now we're flying like
The Angel's on the edge of the night . . .
All right, all right.
And now we're coming to the
Gates of dawn . . .

(Inspired by Meat Loaf and other Metal and Heavy Metal music)

Part 03

Self-Consciousness, Law Of Unification (all bodies)

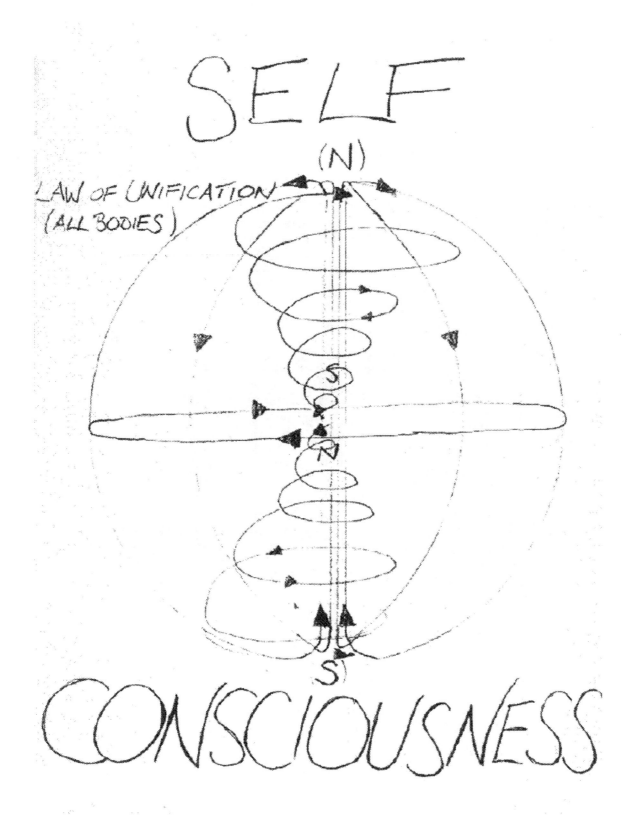

Self-Consciousness

Self-Consciousness:
My guiding principle,
My strength,
It pulls me onward
Into supple embrace
And all I have to do is fall
Into place.

What and where to go to:
The point of no return.
I find events
Beyond my control . . .
Permanent pressures
Not good to destroy.
Therefore,
Go with your flow,
Let yourself go,
Allow for release,
And pressure,
Though it may be hard to distinguish,
Take the time,
To Revelate,
To Concentrate,
What is you.

Of my glory,
Of my shine,
Of my mind,
To be with,
Believe in,
Admire,
Participate,
To Correlate
With some measured attempt
At Beauty,
To Complement,
Supplement
Your reality:
My duty
To the gaps . . .
Contemplate, Demonstrate
Subtle permutations,
To make clear Reality,

Through involvement:
The aspects
Of our Life
Consciousness.

I will continue
This dance,
The window
Of Oppurtunity.
One goal, one desire,
To bring clarity,
Answers
And Embetterment,
Truth,
From Observation and Experience:
The Distinct realm of the Philosopher,
Not to mention the Poet!

(Inspired by all those who know we can learn all things from Observation and Experience.)

Anger

To be consumed by inner passion,
Overidden by uncontrolled emotion,
My senses reel in the midst of battle
As I grasp for my slipping saddle.

My opponent taunting and laughing,
Emotions rise up, cobra's ready to spring,
Feverishly striving to control
An onslaught of damage to my Soul.

Then, to contemplate of this, the cause,
For I wish not to be violent and give evil applause,
Standing to the side, searching for the reason
When I see light dawn behind the treason.

Realizing there is little sense of value
To this, which energy is so devoted . . .
And those snakes without power to lend
Die away . . . and of them is the end.

Friendship

Journeying, as one upon the perfect path,
Combined and bonded in spirit and form.
A relationship bearing no malice,
An affiliation completely beautiful and untorn.

To hold complete understanding,
Comprehending our intricate design.
Of our Love, Hate and Belief,
A Knowledge so cherishingly Divine.

Having TOTAL TRUST towards each other,
A devotion of utter Truth and Parity,
Shining white light silhouettes the two,
Abound in forms of true solidity,
Becoming an everlasting entity.

Unbreakable by evil words or thought,
The true Meaning and Glory of this ULTIMATE Love.

(Inspired by, in many cases, the greater value of Friendship than per se Family,
Marriage or Relationships; can we not just interact as good Friends?)

You Are A

Hello Non-Sequitor Exitor,
Non-Responsive Despondent.
Taking Parable Distribution,
Giving Intangible Connection,
Definitely Uncategorical,
Clearly contradictory,
Uttering utters,
Of indescribables.
No, this is not a compliment,
Shout the fuck up:
Repetitious Orderings.
Unchanging Adaptors,
Playing with the spiral,
Fixed point but no destination,
Bring it around,
To the self-acknowledgement,
Do not stay at Z.

Superstition

Human, you
Must Eliminate
Superstition:
Like up or down
Or through.
One must identify exactly
What things are,
Based on Reality.
Where else?
There is Nothing
Which is not in Reality,
Whether it be
Finite or Infinite,
Inner or Outer,
Real or Virtual,
Universe or Multiverse,
In this Plane or Dimension
Or another . . .
So it might be up or down
Or through . . .
The purpose is, to
Clear up the ambiguity,
Otherwise you are in confusion.
And this gets you Now Here.

(Inspired by the dualistic paradoxes in above theories)

A Little Poem For You . . .

Dear Father,
You Conquered
Cancer,
Allergies, Asthma
And more
With Fasting, Meditation
And Prayer.
Now it is time,
To get rid of your inhibition,
To give yourself a break,
In C to B,
FEAD on the rest,
And the whole alphabet to take.
You have now gained
The plateau you have been fighting for . . .
Yes, you have:
The pendulum has swung
To the other extreme
Somehow balancing out
Past errors and wrongs . . .
You are forgiven,
To the Nth derivative.
Now you can rest . . .
You cannot be in perpetual transition,
And hyper acceleration,
Of upward progression,
With conscious intent,
To the ethereal planes . . .
Go with your momentum,
Do more and it's redundant,
Not to mention bad for the engine . . .
I except you for who you are,
In fact, I admire you,
However, you do not . . .
The bodies are capable of all positions.
In fact, if you do not move around,
You will pop a piston!
So, give yourself a break,
In C to B,
FEAD on the rest,
And then G . . .
You shall sleep peacefully.
For you cannot save the World or Universe,
Only your Self . . .

Cause And Effect

Life is the maintaining of your own,
Death is the sacrifice of your own.

Life is the Circle,
Death is the Spiral.

Life is sustaining,
Death is transition.

Life is expansion,
Death is contraction.

Life is inhale,
Death is exhale.

As you can see we die many times in one life,
As you can see we live many times in one death.

This is why there are the walking dead,
This is why there are the sleeping living.

The only constant is change,
Change is the only constant.

Do not be afraid of Death,
Death does not exist.

He is only terror,
She is only change.

Millions of cells are continually dying and being born in your body every day.

Life and Death are figments of our imagination.

Is Illusion, Illusion being what covers what is beneath.

The trick lies, in discovering, you fool the trick.

So Grasp at the underlying, and you shall see Light.

(Inspired by possibly the greatest God and/or Goddess of them all: Death. We
Pisces are particularly interested in the never answered question of the After Life
for how does anyone ever bring back any evidence or proof)

The Pathway To All Realities

My motivation and purpose is Life and Existence.
Exploring Reality is either terrifying or terribly exhilarating.
To explore Reality we have to get by our instinctive animal urges, the antithesis
Of change, the desire to remain in unconscious flow;
'Don't dare venture into the Unknown!'
Use logic and prediction to prove actual danger to you.
Great levels of Abstraction,
Voyage into Fantasy . . .
Beckon beautiful trees to a better day.
To understand a state, object, subject, yourself, to the opposite,
To obtain a state you must strive for it.
Ode to be invulnerable, never to catch the thorns of fear,
Never to diminish in capability and potential,
Like an untorn child open to the wonders of the Universe.
So much depends on receptivity, so many ways to go astray,
Including not to go astray.
So we might as well better
Explore, take a chance, experiment,
Enter the whirlpool of vast experience,
The interpenetration of realities.
Make the unknown known,
To discover and invent,
And let time work out
The seems, if you are hurt, it will heal,
Let Reality open itself up to you,
There is no reason it won't,
Unless you misuse the knowledge you gain,
Do anything as long as you harm no one,
Just call on your own Will, at any time,
And you'll be fine until you dine,
Now come, to a time far beyond . . .
Echoing over the milestones of forgotten Humanity,
Coursing through the stars of explosive release,
Desire, encroached in your point of no return,
Translate the real to abstract, Reverse,
Again, Extrapolate,
You can know everything,
Do anything,
Place yourself in any Time,
Time is speed of energy,
Place is volume,
They are directly proportionate,
Slow yourself and things go faster,
Fast yourself and things go slower,
This is The Pathway To All Realities.

Self Efficiency

Yea, you must even up
All loose ends
And threads
In Space and Time
To solve all
Your problems . . .
Do not leave
Something hanging,
Lest you end up
Hanging yourself . . .
Do not owe a penny,
Do not have any debts,
Financial, personal, karmic
Or otherwise . . .
Understand the application
Of Metaphysics
To Practice
In mundane activity . . .
Then you will be able
To be less serious,
As there is nothing
You have to seriously take anymore . . .
You will be able
To be open minded,
Interested in Life,
As there is nothing more to hide . . .
No more lies . . .
You will be able
To do whatever you wish,
Free to live,
As you are prohibiting
No one else . . .
You will be an able,
Capable,
Super Duper,
Automobile,
You will be able,
To dream and fly,
As there is no longer
Anything holding you . . .

(Inspired by Pythagoreanism which applies Philosophy to practice in your life)

Sex

Dream on, Dream on,
It is good:
The connection to subconscious
Monstrous Gorgings
In the meadowfields,
Gorgeous monstrosities
In fields of meadows.

Take non-relatives
And marry them,
They become your blood.

Non-sequitors, to good music,
Creates worship.

Make heartbeat music and
You've got an audience.

Music with abstract,
Nice balance.

The apparently meaningless actually is
very meaningful.
It is just a question of going with
the flow . . .

Gorgeous flowing bodies
Coursing over each other . . .

—Wait, such is meaningful, uh, I think I need a point of reference to babble
all around. It is the skill of all great writers . . .

Now, I'm going to write something to my next love; it will be a beautiful Poem:

My next Love,
Will be my Love.

Please my Goddess . . .

Send me a Babe
With a Gorgeous Bod
To my undress,
First Class,

Nice Ass . . .

She will like all my jokes
And be totally loving

        Hey, I like these!

She has blonde hair,
Tragically hip,
Sweet lips (not cherry),
Soft caress.

Bright smile,
Warm embrace,
Freedom flow . . .

Duck waddle,
Goofy stoop,
Toothless grin.

Black eyeglass silhouetted,
Black strap window pane,
Panty liner,
Give me her now!

Peach fuzz, optic shadow,
Suggested promises,
Between the sheets,
Melting, into warm pillow,
Against right leg,
Soft lower support,
Slow, gradual motion,
Lasting long slow
Relaxing orgasm,
Warm embodiment,
Picturesque,
Soft,
Peach fuzz, optic shadow,
Into her breasts,
Lasting sleep . . .

(Inspired by diverse physical attractions, not only the post-German uberhaupt
mensch still dominating all media's)

True Love Is Made

The Sun amidst large rolling white clouds shines its rays onto the Earth. A breeze swaying the broadleaf trees is. The birds play in the wind, their shadows fleeting glimpses upon wood, water, and stone. On this shore of a large pond, a reflection of the motion above circles in warm depths. From wild and free flying creatures to the microscopic bacteria, a paradise teeming with life, the changes flow into one another. With the air scented from abundant field flowers, the bees harvest, the insects hum, and humans socialize and relax. Everything is in continual motion. The little glade grows. It becomes a haven for travelling souls, a place in which to gain Strength and Peace. With this freedom of motion, momentum is gained.

In a circling ball of energy whipping off trails of sparks, they who are here, fly in glory. All becomes appreciated with slow pulsating expansion and contraction beginning . . .

Life's wonders are opened.

Everything glows heat as electricity spins around in crescendos and dimuendos of caressing flame. Flight increases in widening circles. Limitations, inhibitions, fall away, are pulled off, revealing the brilliance of the Universe.

Entering the Vastness of Eternity, the Infinite Power is realized, the fabricated threads of Time disappear, are ripped asunder, and in a blazing roar True Love Is Made.

Hell Is The Denial Of Your Flow (Part I)

To die, to die, my naked pearl jeweled eye,
Would require a view far greater than our sky . . .

Fly by nights of pale azure gold
And reach a place where no one kills
Our children's children anymore.

I would rather wrench my heart right out
Of my gut, than deny the beauty of our world.
So many witness to death. So many wrought
With injustice, stabbed in the back.
They accept the reality of kill and be killed,
It is Nature's way: Look at it!
How can you speak of live and let live?
The audacity . . .

I can speak of live and let live, because
We have suffered enough now.
We have passed the agony of growth now.
It can be the pleasure of growth from
Now on. Our spines have tortured their
Way up. Those who must suffer more will
Pass on. Our spines have become stronger.
Energy can flow easily along them.
We can now live and let live
Because we have achieved civilized Society:

It is now actually possible to live off all the Element's . . .
For we have not just ripped and raped the World
But gained everlasting continual sustainments
Of the basic blocks of our collective fundaments.

(Inspired by the great need and want for sustainable development everywhere)

Hell Is The Denial Of Your Flow (Part II)

I like brisk shaking, rustling tree
Branches. Full scattered blowing, slow
Whispering, heated debate, should I
Hate? Should I skither down into
The core of my being and release its
Opulence to set the situation right?
Trembling heart, do I have you in grasp?
Random energies, what realm do you
Depart to!
Internal turmoil, how can you exist
In such pretty walls?
Diamond casing, why so tight?
5, 4, 3, 2, 1, Magic to be cast tonight!
Fear! Unseen forces move your mind.
We did not do anything to survive:
We are products of Nature.
Fear. Death. What has Death to do?
Death of Ego?
DEATH (Check your heart rate).
DEATH is the ceasing of a,
BIRTH is the beginning of a,
I no longer hold anymore importance to
What I see:
I put no value on these normal cultural
Accepted values. None.
I want to travel the scenery,
Not the people.
Just the scenery.
Are these just my thoughts?
Can I breathe anyway I want? It
Makes sense that I could.
Have the trees stilled with the stilling of
My thought?
Do I really have control of myself?
Are things going on that I do not know?
Have I been doomed forever by a previous
Act?
Have the invisible talons of DEATH finally
Gotten their firm grasp on me?
Do I have no escape?
Am I doomed to repeat the act
Which will put me into an
Ever Increasing Spiral of Death?

Will all my ventures be blocked
As a result of this and will my
Potential never be reached . . .
How did Death get into it?
Or are we talking about
Entrapment, Suffocation,
Imprisonment, Degeneration,
Incapacitation, HELPLESSNESS,
Restriction of your capability to function in . . .
To survive in a positive productive manner,
Here Now.

(Inspired by our innate fear of change, the unknown and how our ignorance leads us to our own personal hell's)

Heart

I have written everything by
Primarily the Heart,
By what *really* is me.
Letting the Pattern resolve itself
And balancing it with
The Common Thread Of Humanity,
I maintain Objectivity
Yet still draw upon my Subjectivity.
What I wish to portray
Then follows.
In neat definite order,
I say what I have to say
To make my point clear
And if nothing ensues
It was never meant to be.
But if in Truth,
A Commonality,
Then what I know
And what I have seen
Can be of benefit
To others,
And free your hearts
From misery.
I have no alterior motive
(I am not the only one),
No selfish greed,
Beyond Recognition for what I Cause,
In Silver Please!
Truly, I wish to discover Truth,
As soon as I can,
I am going to be . . .
A Teacher of Philosophy.

(Inspired by the ever-persistent conundrum in Philosophy and all other fields of the difference between Subjectivity and Objectivity. See also my Evolutionary Essay's.)

The Secret To Happiness Is Now Here

Consider it as a whole,
The more energy you give out,
The more you will receive in return.
All things to Balance.
So now, give yourself a big sigh of relief . . .
The more you feed your environment,
The more it will feed you in return.
It is like glorious Light
Pulsating in return.
In fact, the more you take,
The more you will give out,
So, take a deep breath today.
There is a metaphysical horizon here,
Which everything balances to.
A standing wave pattern,
Is it the horizon, or is it the sun,
For us to ultimately go through?
The sun works exactly in this fashion,
The beauty of fusion,
This balance is a relation
Of all the forces around you,
But what are they?
Each has an exhale and an inhale,
Of equal breadth in return,
Breath in, Counter-Clockwise Spiral,
Breath out, Clockwise Spiral,
The Right Hand Rule,
SCOPE!
A Super Continuum Of Perpendicular Equilibrium,
Forming a Sphere,
From Universe, to World, to Soul,
Two Opposing Spiral Motions
Which can be divided into more,
To cover all Reality,
Thereby, being perfectly stable.
A Sphere is perfectly Symmetrical,
The Potential of each Human.
All Energy works to Balance,
Resulting in Nothing, Zero,
The Circle, Sphere.
Nothing is indestructible,
Nothing is Perfect,
Nothing is Everything in return.

The Balance of Everything is Nothing in return.
All Energy fills a vacuum.
The Universe is a SCOPE
For us to go through,
A Super Continuum Of Perpendicular Equilibrium,
A Vast incredible energy flow
Which is not tangible,
But quite Tangential, Perpendicular.
The Physical Sphere
Needs Nothing in return,
As it is Everything, is perfectly
Stable, the combination
Of two opposite spirals.
The North and South Poles
Are attracted to each other,
Then become one,
And thus, the Universe
Becomes one Force,
Completely onto its own,
A Single product of all realities,
Spiral being the transitional,
Form of using breath, in return,
To natural motion, go to continual,
Infinity, we never die in the physical
Brilliant Central Sun,
The place of perfect balance,
Of all realities, Spirals, converging
Overlapping energy friction,
At One with the rhythmic pulsing
Of the Universe.
Forever.
And all it needs is Nothing . . .
Nothing coursing through it,
It coursing through Nothing,
SCOPE,
In continual motion,
Go through all Timelines . . .
We are presently still evolving,
Racing with the spiral
Of unconscious flow.
In fact, it is these two
Opposing spirals which connect the circular planes,
Just draw it,
Picture it, visualize, try it.
What is true can be seen.
If we can just combine

The two opposing spirals into one Sphere,
As they naturally can,
If we gain closer connection,
To the Sun,
We will copy, replicate, as we are
Products of Nature, even small clones.
The Universe reproduces itself
And become Immortal, Timeless,
Free of all Bondage,
At One with the Sun, with Bliss,
And Nothing more we have to do,
And we can rest in the eternal happiness,
Now Here.

(Inspired by the black and white pen art of this part of Poetry Lore)

Close-Mindedness

It seems . . .
We are just a little extreme,
A little too frantic,
Intense,
Caught up in blind motion,
And then . . .
We cannot remember
When we forgot.
Just a little too extreme,
And harsh,
So harsh on ourselves,
An offspin
Of the Medieval Ages . . .
Too damn serious,
There is a difference,
In Between,
Integral Discipline
And out of control Extremism,
Rigid, unrelaxed,
Patternic, repetitious,
Unconscious, dogmatic
Erratic behavior.
Like, there is only one way
To do something . . .
How about opening your minds
To the multitudinal
Applications of Truth,
And Reality.
And how about Truth while you are at it . . .

Truth

Yes, Truth does exist . . .
To those who deny it,
They are mislead Conformists.
There is Reality.
Are you denying the existence of such a Tree?
Then, thou art crazy.
There is a difference between,
A Tree and a Dog,
Though, they are closely connected,
If you know what I mean . . .
Yes, look at what I mean,
Average the connection.
What is true
To all things?
I will leave this one up to you . . .
And be satisfied,
In revealing,
To you, both an Apple
And an Orange are Fruit.
True, is it not?
All things are Energy,
Truth, my associate,
Is Commonality.
You are well come . . .

(Inspired by light optimists everywhere and the difference between facts, relative truths and absolute Truth)

Embetterment

In attempt for my absolute best,
Striving forward continuously,
As much as possible,
Breathing,
Better,
Grasping for my best,
Breathing,
Better,
With discipline,
Never veering from the practice,
Of the Truth which exists,
No matter how much it takes,
To maintain one's own,
While achieving the Objective,
Perception of what is occuring,
Kinda like chess,
And grasp onto it,
And if it's worth something,
If it is Truth, has Value,
Then apply it to one's life,
No matter how much it takes,
A Truth will give more back.

(Inspired by all those true Theosophists)

Our Mother Goddess, The Full Moon

It is said she guards the way through the portal of the night,
The pathway into the dark forest,
Where not only her lovers have wandered.
In ethereal form they find their way
To her den. She-Who-Guards-The-Night
And walks secret and hidden amongst Human,
Sometimes growling in her fevered glory,
With her fine supple body and her long black hair,
She does indeed prefer her lovers breathing and living,
Even suffering, for we are only in the state between states,
Not quite awake not quite sleeping . . .
Wonder at her moonlit phosphorescent water side,
Taking in the energy there for all Man and Woman to partake of,
While we keep nulling and calling out to her
Unprecedented infinite spirit cycles already,
And I cry in grey silver wolf form, "Arrroooooo, arr-arr-arrrooooooo . . ."
We died and went to the Heavens, for she,
Mother Goddess, The Full Moon,
Brought us plenty of Shadow Energy too,
And now we sit, with a little smile,
Afterwards in the silver fire of the residual glow of deep pleasure . . .
Thankful we did not drink too much from her ever-flowing fountain of life itself,
Of here subtleties, while she continues walking quietly and silently amongst us
In her many choices of ethereal bodies
And in her great fervor to inspire all nearby . . .
With her dense moist fields of energy in the air,
We dance on the sands of timelessness,
Grateful so much has been bestowed upon us
In her invincible magical embrace.
Shall we ever be at her very same level,
face-to-face with her shining silver love,
Or is it in fact already a perpetual
Quantum existential reality, and we must
Reach out a hand to touch such Energy,
For even the veil of the monk is not fully concealed.
Hopefully, we shall never tempt her wrath again.
And protect our own hearts, bodies, minds and spirits,
Drinking from the very same essence in reality itself.
We shall never forget again we are immortal, already too,
Though only in Spirit and Soul and thank her once again,
For all she has given us, Our Mother Goddess, The Full Moon,
She-Of-Many-Faces, She-Who-Guards-The-Night,
The-She-Wolf-Who-Guards-The-Night-And-Preys-Upon-Human,
The pathway into the forest, beware her wraith too, then to her wane,
Where only her lovers in ethereal form have made it to . . .

Truth Is Commonality

All things discovered, in Truth,
Are Real, in Nature,
Earth, Water, Air and/or Fire,
And Ether, N Light,
Are Elementary my dear, Watch On!,
Like Clockwork, they arrive,
The Four Horsemen of the Apocalypse,
And then Armageddon,
The Eradication of all Evil
On a continual basis, each day,
Holding within them, all other elements,
Behaving in the same fashion, all ways,
As the Element's, of Nature in Reality,
Create Polarity, and Convergence,
In continual Flow, and Stability,
Forever on the Finite, Infitudinal,
Spherical Continuum, the Universe,
You can now Real Eyes . . .
In the end Good and Truth will surpass.

(Inspired by the Delphi Oracle, Prophecies and Doomsday Prophecies in many
Philosophy's and Religion's i.e. the most dramatic being the biblical Armaggedon
triggered by the death of the third Anti-Christ coinciding approximately with the end
of the Mayan Calendar resulting in the rise of their Fire Earth Serpent God who is
equivalated with Satan; thus 2011 and 2012 . . . Good, however, driven by Truth
shall always win in the end and is it not: 'The end of the world *as we know it'* and
do they not just write their *own* self-fulfilling prophecies? Do we not write each of
our own futures? So, this poem is also inspired by REM)

Evolution To Self-Consciousness

Oh, dear Parents,
Don't be disparing!
It's a fact, your Children
Know much more than you . . .
How, can it be
All you have learned
And struggled and toiled for
Your Child already knows!
And, they are lecturing you now
On the ways of the World,
Reposé, Upward grasp,
Downward thrust, disarmé!
Could it be you taught them everything?
Of course! Is this not what you intended?
Children start with what you have ended,
'From all end comes new beginning.'
We are what you are and more,
We are improving,
Making things better,
Faster, stronger, we are evolving.
From amoeba, two amoeba, too amoeba,
To plant, two plant, too plant,
To animal, two animal, too animal,
To human, two human, too human.
Each more capable than the last,
Everything before achieved, maintained,
Inborn, to grasp upward in quest
Of the next circle of completeness.
To self-consciousness,
To health,
To wealth,
To freedom.
A random twirling of energy,
Matters interweaving,
Spiralling from form to form,
Circling over and over again.
Until it is so familiar,
You, yourself, discover,
A reflection of sufficient
Energy, in a pool of water.
Ah, it has just begun, again,
Then you gain seperation
From communal conception,

Justice Children growing . . .
No longer an animal, you are human,
The realm of self-consciousness,
Discovering you are unique,
Capable of Objective Perception.
Of Observation and Experience:
Learning,
The Way,
To health,
To wealth,
To freedom.
And this is why
Human's can do the things they do,
Because we are still semi-conscious,
Still part animal.
Predator and prey interrelation,
The instincts of the animal
Are random reactionary fluctuations,
For the sake of such animal.
How much is now explained,
All the devestation
Is because, though appearing to be a human,
Is actually not yet, by Evolution, fully Human . . .
And then we will meet the Alien . . .
And find out how similar we are
In the evolution throughout the Universe
In this Timeline . . .

(Inspired by Theory's of Evolution proposed by many)

Society

ACT 1: (this will be done on stage, screen or by 3D Holographic imagery)

Scene 1: A fence on the edge of a sunset with a person with big hands and a little head, on the edge, picking his nose. Though his head is about the size of a baseball, his nose is large. With no apparent sequence of logical events, a baseball comes zooming across the field and soundly nails him in the head. He falls over the edge and out of view.

Scene 2: A blue sky bright over a definitely alien but somewhat earth-like World. A moon in the sky on the left horizon. A large plain with a long river is seen which disappears into the edge of the sharp rocks of the mountain passageway which dominates the picture. A rough edge shows a large drop off on which comfortably a bearded dwarf with a metal horned helmet and otherwise brown cloaked body (4' 4") is leaning against, with one arm. A mule is standing bored to the left. All of a sudden from behind some large rocks a huge ugly ogre (humanoid monster) leaps up growling and throws over its head, two-hander style, a boulder the size of the dwarf, into the Dwarf. He falls over the edge and out of view.

Scene 3: In a full house spectacle of Arthurian people, 2 gallant knights dressed in blazing white armor are charging towards each other. Their lances flute honorable Heraldry indeed. The crowd becomes an unfocused blob and only the intense stare of horses nostrils is seen. A side view show the two knights colliding, one breaking his lance and one toppling out of view.

Scene 4: A game of Polo is in progress with various shots of action. It is apparent the greens are winning. In a desperate attempt to regain some points, the reds struggle back en force and gain momentum. In the rush of action one red breaks free towards the goal and in a shout of defiance aims for the skittering ball with a tremendous blow. She misses. She topples out of sight into a black hole which has just appeared below her.

Act 2: (the lighting is dim, diffused yet still very visible)

Scene 1: Seated in a rough circle on four stone benches are three figures. There is a name tag in front of each of the stone benches. The three figures are quite different than each other. One is the dwarf, the other the knight, the other the small head. The rest of the picture is black and light in torches only illuminates the area. The stonework looks modern. From their voices it seems to be a very high ceiling in a wide chamber which they are in; depth of sound in the area is noticeable. They are viewing each other suspiciously. The Dwarf and knight are standing with weapons drawn questioning each other. The small-head is dumbfounded. At the height of the dwarf and knight's now-argument-about-to-become-melee a large zap with a ripping flash explodes between the two. The amazingly sexy polo Woman falls very clumsily out of the air onto a stone bench backward (in the play she will pop out of a trapdoor). In a disheveled squawk she falls to the ground. The knight immediately goes to help her, the dwarf makes a sign and mutters an oath against Magic, the small-head raises an eyebrow—we see their names are Gurhard (Small-head), Dim (Knight), Ellebena Levenena (Polo Woman), Johnson (Dwarf).

Scene 2: (After raising his eyebrow Gurhard goes into a monologue)
Gurhard: Well, character sketches are reacting consistently to their stimuli but our situation is still mysterious. It might be we are here because we all died and by nature of our demises, if I can assume we died in the same manner, or we are going to be put on trial again for the crimes of humanity, or we are inextricably connected by some common factor and so we are here, maybe our deaths . . . Or some alien force has brought us here for questioning. Or, we are here to demonstrate our capabilities to sociate. Maybe, we subconsciously choose to be here and play this scene out. Personally, I think the writer of this script has brought us together to reveal satirical comment on society . . . (he raises his eybrow and cocks his head to the audience)
Dwarf: Yah, no kidding, ay . . .
Then a subdued silence overcomes the scene. Elebeena Leveneena gets up and they all hold hands. This is done naturally and they all begin to prance around in a circle. A great dancing music fulls the hall and the players are lost in dance.

Scene 3: They all embrace each other and then in tears, sorrow about how empty their lives are. The look at each other dejectedly;
Johnson: You know I have always wanted to dance like that (he flicks away a tear, now fully composed).
Ellebeena Leveneena: I know. Aaah! (in great anguished sorrow)
Gurhard: I understand it helps.
Dim: I have never enjoyed that. But this time . . .
Ellebeena Leveneena: I know!
Dwarf: I know!
Gurhard: Why is it that everybody knows?
Dim: I know.
They then all say together: Forgive me, for I have dined . . . (they then all kneel down and raise their arms to the sky, in singing pounding chant, with Johnson keeping the beat):

Oh holy one, oh.
Oh oh ohhh,
Oh holy one, we wish you
The best
On your holy trip . . .

(The melodic resonant digital crescendo descends to lowly speech levels. Twangs of sadness and disharmony are heard in the background)

Goodnight.

Scene 4: The four humans are now sleeping the long sleep of death which is peaceful but also very sad. This is portrayed by the "sleepers".

Scene 5: Standing, looking into some invisible imaginery scene in front of her, a fog has arisen. As she talks, the other three rise up and circle around her with their bodies and arms moving up and down in rhythm. A rhythmical African drum beat keeps them steady. The mist is swirled and thrown upward.

Ellebeena Levennena: (She snarls and her eyes widen) Begone cursed one, cowl back to those depths from whence you came!

Begone foul beast trying to enslave me . . . Begone! (In a scream, the other's have stopped now, the drums have crescendoed)

Dim, Johnson, Gurhard: Begone!! (the drumming continues and then descends into nothing. They return to their slumber state. The scene blackens.)

Act 3: (There remains a faint trace of mist which quickly dissipates)

Scene 1: The scene lightens into twilight. The members are still asleep except for Johnston, the dwarf, who sitting on the edge of one of the stone benches looks down at the audience (cause the whole stage raised up), glugs a beer, and begins.

Johnston: You know . . . I always felt small and unworthy you know . . . I had to up my defenses. So, I became stolid, strong, stable . . . skilled in ways of war, battle, workmanship, engineering . . . Confidence. (He looks away) Power! (He throws his helmet in fury into the audience) Look at those foolish ones . . . (Pointing to sleeping comrades)

Pain, Doubt, Fear! They sleep despite of it all, some caught in its feeling, even in sleep, the pervading condition of human, to be grabbed in by such a reckless monster of emotion. They feel nothing but it. I feel none of it. I feel none of it. I made myself strong, as a mule, strength to carry any rock, back to hold any mountain and no tears to speak of (To audience): Do you understand? You! (pointing to individual male member of audience, who looks somewhat insecure) Do you? Huh? Do you! Answer me! (he continues this until someone answers, negatively or positively) I don't! (or) I don't either!

Hah hah hah hah hahaha . . . (Screeching heavy metal guitar riffs hit the audience, then fades with his continuous laughter which increases to a cackle as the lights fade to blackness.)

Scene 2: (Blackness. Voices between Dim and Johnston)

Johnston: Yo stupid. Wake up.

Dim: Huh? Unnhh. What do you mean?

Johnston: Up! Up you dolt. And make it good, eh!

Dim: What . . . Oh yah! (There is a few moments of total blackness and silence, then a huge visual and audio explosion of light is shot up/beamed up from the floor, four beams around him, which all then immediately blackens and then fades into a rumble of drums.

(blackness)

Johnston: Not bad . . . now stop bothering us man and let me sleep.

Into the light, with his helmet off, hair softly down his neck, Dim is looking up at the sky above the audience (the stage has lowered again below the audience and the sky is an actual 3D Holographic Projection above the audience) with one hand held up with a thoughtful and philosophical look on his face. His one foot is on the bench, too. He then drops them both but keeps his head up. He then turns and places his helmet on one of the stone benches. This has all been done calmly, relaxed. Then, changing his mind, he takes the helmet and rests his hands on it between his legs as he sits down.

Dim: I have always liked such a pose . . . It makes me imagine I can reach up and touch space. Somehow, reach and up and . . . My goal in life is to perfect such a pose. I have never perfected it and I don't think I will until the day I die . . .

(The light up to this point had approached a near squint and after 'die . . .' it deftly pops out)

Dim: (In a pause after waiting for something . . . The stage remains dark, at the backstage is heard some wires moving, something bangs to the floor, a curse is heard, there is definitely something wrong with the stage here . . . It looks like some technical problems. Several lights flicker and turn on as though being tested. They are all the wrong ones.

Basically, the audience has to be convinced a technical problem occured. The audience lights go up. 'Dim' looks questioningly about, definitely out of character, then quickly recovers getting back into his 'Dim' character. But then the stage producer walks on stage and 'Dim' falls away again.

Stage Manager (to audience): We are sorry for this, we are terribly sorry (he is terribly nervous) Ahhh, I don't know how to put this, but there has been a terrible accident (he has a british accent) in the back and we are afraid there will be a delay.

Dim (in character): Hey, don't worry about it, we will continue like . . . (Just then, one of the stage techinicians at the back of the stage touches a couple of wires in place and "BOOM!" he electrocutes himself. This is quite noticeable to the audience. It also raises the three others to quick attention (they are still in character though). The stage technician stumbles on stage, smoking heavily from his whole body with a cigarette on fire in his hand, and falls dead to the ground just as all the stage lights are put back on.

Stage Manager: Wohhh . . . It works! (He then smiles at Dim) The show must go on! (The lights are then in their proper sequence, highlighting Dim, shadowing the three sleepers, and the dead worker lights up. Dim is sleeping, too.)

He is content and so are the others.

End

(Inspired by Godot and Shakespeare and how to stop smoking)

Two Scientists Outside a Building With 4 Inlaid Water Fountains, 366 Doors, 25 Windows, People Inside and Out, 2 Storeys, 5 Pigeons, One Cat, 2 Solar Collectors, 3 Radio Antennaes, Many Compterized Automations and An Urinal.

"Oh Despair. My insides is about to do a 'Coooop Dehooores'."

"Be reticent fool. If you persist in speaking such petulant phrases, at least favor us with correct spelling and grammar. Oh! How hurtful to the lobes. A twang of disharmony, a twinge of my nerves and you succumb to my twine, quickly away with a little twinkle."

"Ahhh . . . You do me honor with your twisting tongue. But please, respite from such vicious resonance. It is not conflict we want, or need for such matters; I am simply sick: Resolution in such reaction is completely relevant to my internal rearing and roaming. Oh, rant I do raucousness, racking the remains of my once wholesome being. Sad, there is but raunchiness, a rock of sorciphol, clinging and resisting, on my raving gut. Intestines, Colon, Gut, it is only gut now, now a revealing recital of Nature. A grave reprimand. I was and am ruttish with black aura. And I suffer, oh I suffer . . ."

"You have such eloquence. May Blake come back again . . . Your even temperment, deliciously strange, discords reverbrate throughout. Oh, I do not wish to see any closer, your insides. Spare me . . ."

"Spare you I shall! It is now time, anyways, for more casual banter."

"Yes. Restrain from me the foulness of within, it shows all of you and I rather be external from such affairs."

"I say, casual, you touch my thought and only yourself can now decide. Be it relaxed or strained? I tell you siftings, I am stuck in gore. You relate to it and all too well . . . But enough!"

"Yes. Enough."

"Let's chat."

"Let's."

"What about?"

"Oh, anything."

"Anything . . ."

"Yes. Anything . . ."

"Well, today they said there was an explosion at the Nuclear Plant in . . ."

"No, not such. Too violent."

"Yes, you're right. Too violent."

"Did you hear, the Sperm Whale has finally . . ."

"No. You already told me . . ."

"Oh yes, I remember."

"Guess what? They've discovered another form of cancer . . ."

"Please stop. No more. Let's go. I must excrete."

"Yes. Time to return. But you're right, first excrete."

"Yes. Excrete our thoughts."

"Let's."

"Yes."

(Inspired by Blake and Baron and the need for a sense of humor)

You Have To Fight For Freedom

I am Back!
You got to Strive
To Survive,
To Thrive,
To Live.
It does not matter what
You Strive at.
Though, if it's not what you want
You won't be able to.
You have to Strive.
Waiting is futile,. . .
If you Strive
You will be able to Survive,
To Thrive,
To Live.
Striving can be Painful:
It is the Fight For Freedom.
You will have more Pain
If you don't
Push up through the Pain.
The Pain brings Oxygen
Back to the Muscles,
Energy Breaking Down
The Mucous; the Oppression,
Divulging Information,
Gaining the Evolution,
Up through the Pain,
To a Higher Plane,
Of Greater Personal Freedom,
Not to mention Satisfaction.
Strive upwards!
Then why can you not?
You cannot, you cannot, you cannot,
Why not?
Why can you not use the Energy?
You need to Strive.
Why do you die?
Why do you give up
In vain desperation,
Sadness, torment, anguish,
And fall into the pits of depression?
Shrouded now your pale visage,
And destroying all clarity,

Endless maze of confusion,
Delusion, intrusion, then diffusion . . .
Why?
Well my Friend, one thing:
Malnutrition, Starvation,
Desperation,
All things Grow Up.
They Fight For Freedom,
Against Gravity,
To the Sun,
Evolution,
Until Self-Consciousness,
Then you can Strive,
To Survive,
To Thrive,
To Live,
And Break On Through
To The Entire Universe . . .

(Inspired by our personal and collective struggles in the Evolution Of Humanity)

Freedom

The rocks grow easier, flashing
beneath me, I touch them only
with touches, brief powerful
surges which propel me forward
through this sharp blue sky
with perfect white clouds shining
off of the Sun, but they are not the
only ones, this I cross over
in bounds and leaps, it is all
around, spread out before, behind,
to the left, to the right, the rocks
of sharp, biting, killing edges,
they whip below me, I am
gaining momentum to fly off
their very edge, they are rising,
ahead of me a vast plane
of rising rock, to an edge,
to an edge, to an edge, they
all go to an edge and this is
the edge I am going to jump
off with speed and intent into
the incredibly blue, white blue
sky, into its magnificence,
yet upon it, beyond reason,
beyond doubt, contradiction,
possibility, impossibility, finitude
and infinitude: The Universe allows
for all and I will soar,
blasting through the sky, curving
my backward flowing silver wings . . .

(Inspired by Dragon's in the Cosmos)

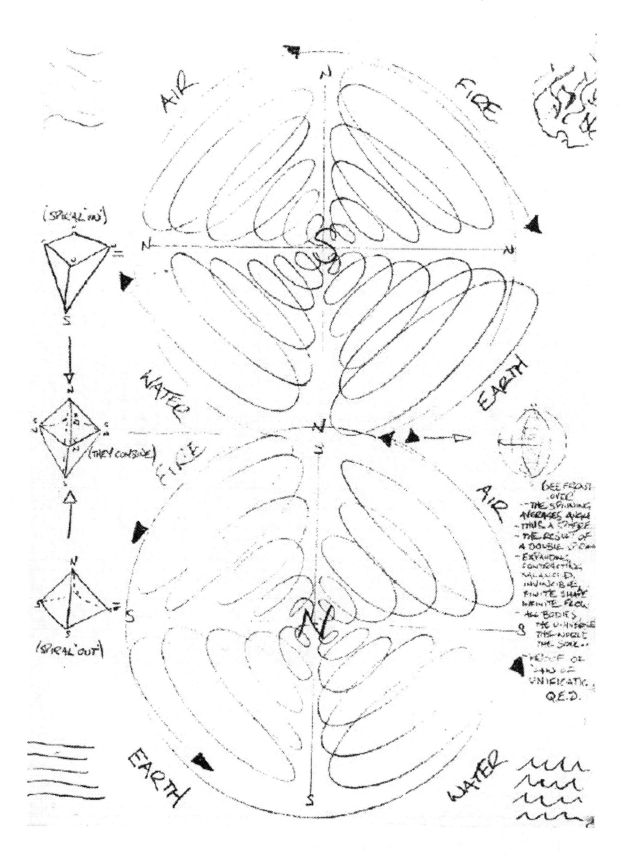